Sew Simple Pinea

Karin Hellaby

Quilters Haven

Publications

About the author

Karin Hellaby is the owner of a quilt shop, Quilters Haven, in Suffolk UK. She is a graduate Textiles teacher who enjoys travelling and giving classes all over the world. As well as writing books, Karin has contributed articles to all the UK quilting magazines.

Karin Hellaby

Karin is an adviser for Arena Travel (www.arenatravel.com), a specialist holiday company that has arranged holidays for quilters in Europe and America. In 1998 Karin was the winner of the Michael Kile Scholarship, and International Retailer of the Year.

Karin feels her greatest achievement is to bring up three sons on her own. She started writing books to help support them through University. Ross and Jason are now enjoying the world of work and Alexander has just started at Swansea University.

Acknowledgements

My thanks to Pam, Debs, Annie, Teresa, Claire, Georgie, Helen, Julia, Nicola, Rosemary and Allan.

This book is dedicated to my current staff. After publishing *Attic Windows* I told them I would not embark on another book for at least a year.

Only a few months later, I asked them to help with *Pineapple Plus*. They embraced the challenge enthusiastically and stitched away making quilts ready for my deadlines. Thank you! Without your help this book would not have emerged so quickly!

First published by
Quilters Haven Publications in 2010

Copyright © Karin Hellaby 2010

Graphics by Rosemary Muntus
Layout by Allan Scott
Photography by Anna McCarthy

Printed by Midas Press

ISBN 978-09540928-7-0
Quilters Haven Publications
68 High Street, Wickham Market
Suffolk IP13 0QU, UK
Tel: +44 (0)1728 746314/746275
E-mail: quilters.haven@btinternet.com

www.karinhellaby.com
www.quiltershavenpublications.com
www.quilters-haven.co.uk
www.blog.quilters-haven.co.uk

Pineapple Plus

In 2008 I published *Sew Simple Pineapple* to explain my way of sewing traditional pineapple patchwork more simply. It caused a sensation in the quilting world. It was both hilarious and flattering to watch jaws drop as I demonstrated the technique to a room full of experienced quilters. There just had to be potential to take my pineapple method further, and I began to design new quilts which could be made as simply as before.

In Pineapple Plus I have explored the use of fabric triangles to replace some of the squares. This has helped to make quilts which use a greater variety of fabrics and colour.

'Quilt as you go' is very popular, so I have included a pineapple version which incorporates the triangles and squares, quilting each block as it increases in size, and ideal for those who do not enjoy working with a large quilt.

This book takes you through three different quilt techniques but the inspirational variations will give you plenty of ideas to make so many more! Enjoy!

The majority of quilts in this book are between 45 and 50 inches square. If you are thinking

Pineapple Plumes *by Pam Bailey*
(48½" square, 9½" block).

about making a single bed quilt (USA twin) then you would just double the fabric quantities and make twice the number of blocks. For a king size quilt you would make four times the number of blocks.

Getting started

Please read before starting a pineapple block!

In Pineapple Plus it is essential to be able to cut accurate fabric squares. A quick method for rotary cutting squares is to cut a strip of fabric and then cut into squares.

When cutting squares into triangles, lay a ruler diagonally from corner to corner and cut. When cutting four triangles make two diagonal cuts without moving the pieces between cuts.

Make sure your sewing machine is in good working order and that you have both a ¼" patchwork foot and a walking foot ready. I like to insert a new needle into my machine whenever I start to stitch a new quilt.

As you stitch the quilt blocks you will alternate between stitching squares and triangles.

When stitching the squares you can use chain piecing. Feed each unit through without breaking the thread. When complete, cut them apart at the chain thread join. Then start stitching again with the first seam lying at the top each time.

A fine marked line is needed for accurate cutting. Use a propelling pencil or a fine Chaco chalk pen (Clover). Then pinch the uppermost layer and make a small nick right on the centre line. Using pointed scissors, cut along the marked lines right up to the stitching.

To stitch the triangles, pin each one well using flower pins at right angles to the block sides. The triangles must meet each other in the centre; lining up with the block sides is less important. Sew each block individually using the 'needle down' facility to turn the corners accurately.

When pressing, you can use spray starch or 'Best Press' to achieve a flat look.

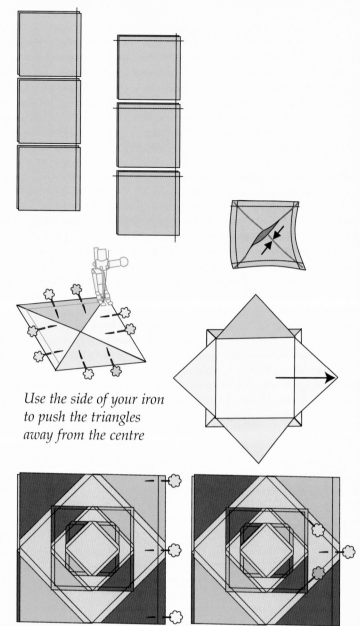

Use the side of your iron to push the triangles away from the centre

Once all your pineapple blocks are complete, stitch them together with a ½" seam. This is where I change to a walking foot on the machine and move the needle position until I use the edge of the foot as a guide. I also use the larger seam when stitching the blocks into rows and rows into the quilt top. This helps to give the quilt a traditional pineapple look. Remember to use the same larger seam allowance when adding the first border.

When sewing the blocks together match the seams accurately. The edges are on the bias, so care is needed. Lay the blocks on a flat surface, right sides together. Pin the corners first, then pin at the centre where the 'pineapple corners' match. It may help to pin each diagonal seam along the sewing line. Pin every 2" and consider stitching with a walking foot. Iron the ½" seams open between the blocks.

Stay stitch the quilt edge by stitching ⅛" before adding the borders to prevent the bias edges stretching.

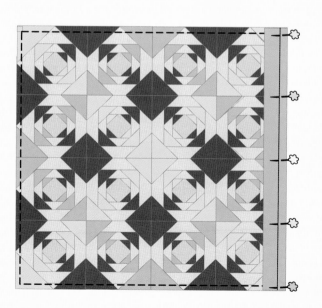

Fabric quantities for several quilts, copies of the diagrams, and yardages for *Stonehenge Stars, Pineapple Plumes, Pineapple Jazz* and *Bubblegum* are all available on the Quilters Haven Publications website at www.quiltershavenpublications.com.

Above: Bubblegum *by Karin Hellaby (38″ × 48″) made from a Layer Cake (10″ squares).*

Below: Pineapple Blues *by Helen Hazon (26½″ square).*

Right: Jack Frost *by Teresa Wardlaw (33½″ square quilt as you go).*

5

Two Triangle Method

These instructions explain how to make one block using the two triangle method. This method was used in the nine blocks forming the centre of the *Rural Jardin* quilt.

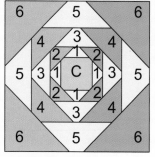

Cutting table

centre	1st	2nd*	3rd	4th*	5th	6th*
3½″	3½″	4¼″	5¼″	6½″	8½″	9½″

* Cut two different colours (here red and blue) giving enough to make two blocks

1 **Centre and First Round.** Mark an X on the wrong side of 3½″ first round square. Place right side down onto the centre square. Pin and stitch round all four sides using a ¼″ seam.

Pull the two squares apart at the centre. Finger crease the top square along one marked line. Make a small cut through the marked square along the marked line. Insert scissors between the squares and carefully cut along the lines to each corner, making sure you only cut through the marked square. Press the triangles away from the centre square.

Trim away excess fabric 'ears' after this and each successive stage.

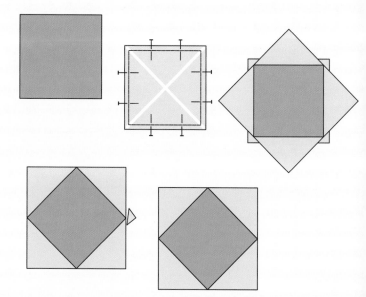

2 **Second Round.** Mark one diagonal line on the wrong sides of each of the different coloured 4¼″ squares, from corner to corner. (Red and blue were used here.) Cut each into two triangles using one diagonal cut from unmarked corner to corner.

Place two triangles, one from each colour, right side down on a previously sewn centre square. The triangles should butt together in the centre, and may be slightly smaller than the underneath square. Pin well. Stitch the square with a ¼″ seam around all four sides.

Cut along the marked line on triangles, again up to the stitching. Press the triangles away from the centre square.

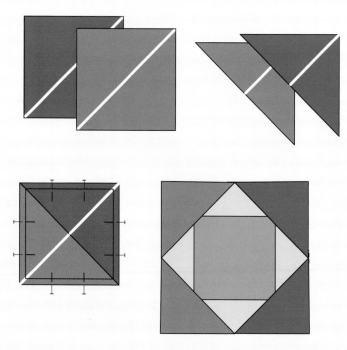

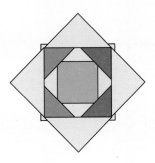

3 **Third Round:** repeat step 1, but this time using a 5¼" square.

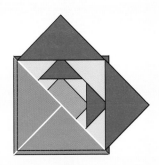 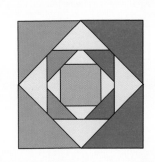

4 **Fourth Round:** repeat step 2, using a 6½" red and blue square to create your triangles. Make sure you follow the colour sequence when pinning.

5 **Fifth Round:** repeat step 1 using an 8½" square. This time stitch with a ½" seam as it produces a more 'pineapple' look. Then trim to a 9½" square, making sure you centre the design.

6 **Sixth Round:** repeat step 2, using a 9½" red and blue square to create your triangles. Again stitch with a ½" **seam**.

Fabric required for a 48″ × 48″ quilt, 10¾″ finished block size

Centre: ¼ yard

Light: 2½ yards (10 fat quarter yards)

Blue: 1 yard (or 4 fat quarter yards)

Red: 1 yard (or 4 fat quarter yards)

Red border: ½ yard or two fat quarter yards

Binding: ½ yard

Cutting the fabrics

Centre: cut 13 × 3½″ squares. Nine squares are needed for centre blocks and four squares for the border cornerstones.

Light Fabrics: cut 13 × 3½″ squares, nine × 5¼″ squares, nine × 8½″ squares. Cut four 2½″ strips in light fabrics for first border. Cut 80 light 2½″ × 5″ rectangles for final border.

Blue fabrics: cut seven × 4¼″ squares, five × 6½″ squares, five × 9½″ squares.

Red fabrics: cut seven × 4¼″ squares, five × 6½″ squares, five × 9½″ squares. Cut four 2½″ strips in red fabrics for second border.

Assembling the quilt

Make the nine blocks at the centre as described on pp 6–7, then add borders as follows.

First border: cut 4 × light 2½″ strips and attach to all 4 quilt sides, using a ½″ seam.

Second border: cut 4 × 2½″ red strips and attach to all four quilt sides.

Final border: stitch the 80 rectangles together to make four borders and attach two to the quilt sides. Stitch four cornerstone pineapple blocks, trim to 5″ and attach to top and bottom borders before stitching borders to quilt.

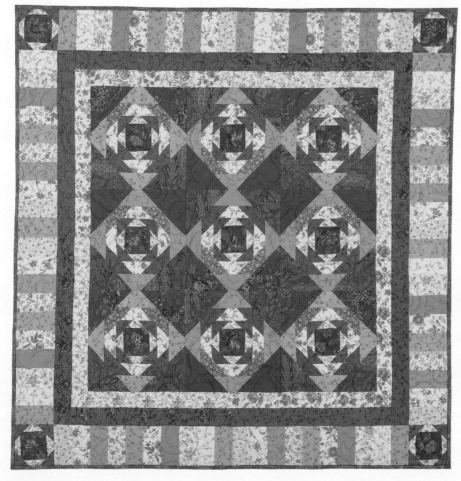

Rural Jardin *(left) by Karin Hellaby (48½″ square, 10¾″ block), centre block (top) and corner block (above).*

Top: Barely Pineapple by Helen Hazon (42½″ square).

Middle: Misty by Julia Reed (40″ square).

Bottom: Pineapple Strippy by Claire Norman (53½″ square).

Left: Two further ideas using the two triangle method, here with just five rounds rather than six – and with some colour variations.

9

Four Triangle Method

These instructions explain how to make one block using the four triangle method. This method was used in the sixteen blocks forming the centre of the *Garden Song* quilt.

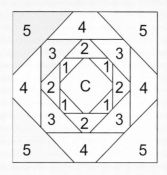

centre	1st*	2nd	3rd*	4th	5th*
3½"	3½"	4¼"	5¼"	6¾"	8¾"

*   Cut four different colours (here pink, blue, yellow and green) giving enough triangles to make four blocks

1   **Centre and First Round:** Cut each 3½" coloured square into four triangles using two diagonal cuts from corner to corner.

Place four triangles, one from each colour, right side down on a centre square. The triangles should meet in the centre. Pin well. The remaining triangles can be used to create three more blocks. Stitch each square with a ¼" seam around all four sides

Press triangles away from centre square. Spray starch if necessary. Trim away any fabric 'ears'.

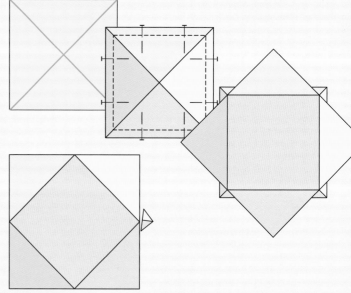

2   **Second Round:** Mark an X on the wrong side of the 4¼" square. Place it face down onto the previously sewn square. Pin and stitch around all four sides, making sure you stitch from the new square side.

Pull the two squares apart at the centre. Finger crease the centre of one marked line and make a small cut through the marked square along the marked line. Insert scissors between the squares, and carefully cut along the lines to each corner, making sure you only cut through the marked square. Press the triangles away from the centre square. Trim away fabric 'ears'.

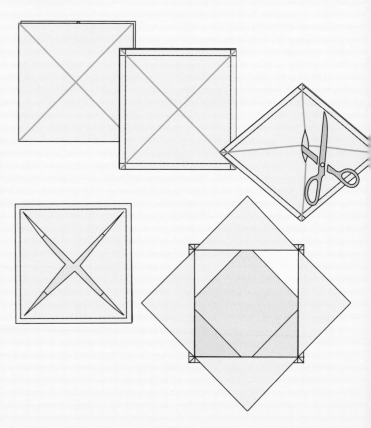

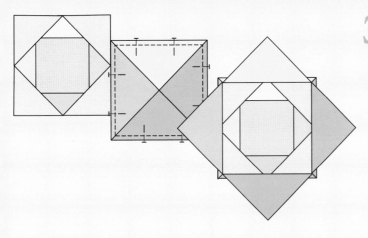

3 **Third Round:** Cut each 5¼" coloured square into four triangles, using two diagonal cuts from corner to corner. Place four triangles, one from each colour, right side down on the centre square, following the previous colours. Pin well. Repeat, making sure that the colour sequence is the same on each block.

Stitch each square with a ¼" seam around all four sides. Press triangles away from centre squares and trim away fabric 'ears'.

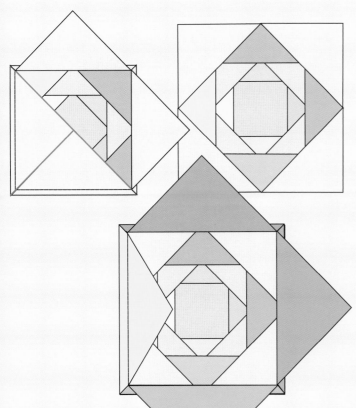

4 **Fourth Round:** Repeat step 2 with a 6¾" square.

5 **Fifth Round:** repeat step 3 with the 8¾" coloured squares, cutting each of them into four triangles.

6 Stitch this block with ½" **seams** to create the 'pineapple' look.

16 blocks, rotated as below, are used to make the Garden Song quilt.

A	A	A	A
A	A	A	A
A	A	A	A
A	A	A	A

11

Fabric required for a 47″ × 47″ quilt, 10″ finished block size

Light: 1¾ yards

Centre diamonds: ¼ yard

Pink, blue, green and yellow: for each colour use ¾ yard of one fabric or three fat quarters.

Cutting the fabrics

Light fabric: for border, cut four 4½″ × 62″ wide strips (parallel to selvedge). From the remaining fabric cut 16 × 4¼″ squares and 16 × 6¾″ squares; for centre, cut 16 × 3½″ squares.

Pink, blue, green, yellow fabrics: cut four × 3½″ squares from each colour (16 squares), four × 5¼″ squares from each colour (16 squares), and four × 8¾″ squares from each colour (16 squares).

Prairie Points: cut 8 × 5″ squares from each colour (32 squares).

Assembling the quilt

Make the sixteen blocks at the centre as described on pp. 10–11, stitch together as shown in the diagram on p. 11.

Border: stitch border strips to quilt and mitre corners.

Prairie points: made from 4½″ squares, each is folded twice diagonally. Arrange the prairie points along the border edge.

Bind with 2½″ light strips.

Garden Song *by Karin Hellaby (47½″ square, 10″ block, 4″ border)*

Detail from Garden Song *showing prairie points*

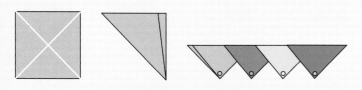

1 After sewing your blocks together and adding any borders, iron the top carefully and place on backing and wadding. Pin together or baste, quilt and trim to remove excess material. Now add embellishments such as the prairie points in *Garden Song*.

2 Cut enough 2½″ wide binding strips to go all the way around the quilt, plus approximately 18″. Join the strips together with a 45° angle seam and press seams open. When using a multi-fabric binding, simply mitre the strips at the short ends before using. Fold the binding in half, wrong sides together, and press. Cut the beginning of the binding at a 45° angle.

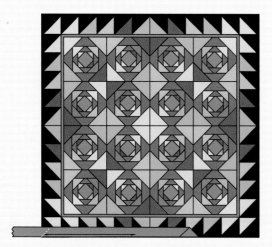

3 Start sewing the binding half way along the bottom edge. Pin in place, but only start stitching 7″ from the beginning of your binding. Use a ¼″ seam allowance and, ideally, a walking foot when stitching the binding to the front of the quilt.

4 Stop sewing ¼″ from the next corner and backstitch to secure the threads. Remove quilt from machine and cut the threads. Fold fabric away from the quilt diagonally. Then fold it back, so the edge lies parallel to the next edge. Sew down the side to the next corner. Repeat for all four corners.

You need to fold the quilt top out of the way to sew the tails together

Fold binding back and sew in place

5 When you get to the last side, end your stitching with a securing stitch 7″ away from the start point. Work with the quilt on a large flat table. Open up the binding and lay the beginning over the end. Mark exactly where they meet. Now make a second mark on the end tail ½″ away from the first mark (this is the seam allowance). From this second mark cut the tail end at a 45° angle. Take both ends, lift and position right sides together, pin and stitch with a ¼″ seam. Press the joining seam open and refold. The binding will now lie flat along the quilt. Complete the binding by turning the folded strip over the edges and hemming.

Quilt As You Go

These instructions explain the method used in the sixteen blocks which make the *Winter Comfort* quilt.

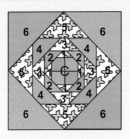

centre	1st	2nd*	3rd	4th*	5th	6th*
3½″	3½″	4¼″	5″	6¼″	8″	9¾″

* Cut two different colours (here green and red) giving enough to make two blocks. The centre block can be made from four 2″ squares, as below.

1 Cut a 13″ square of cotton wadding. Mark two diagonal lines from corner to corner and another two lines across the square from halfway down each side. These lines will help you to align the fabric.

Place the wadding on the wrong side of a 13″ backing square, with the marked lines facing up. Pin or spray baste to attach.

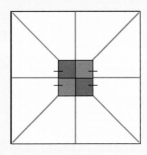

2 **Centre and First Round:** in this example the centre 3½″ square is made from two 2″ red and green squares (above right). Place this right side up on the wadding, using the marked lines to centralise it.

Mark an **X** on the wrong side of a 3½″ patterned square. Place it right side down on the four-patch. Pin and stitch around all four sides. Start and finish in the centre of one side. This will give a 'square' quilting look to the reverse side.

Pull the two layers apart at the centre. Finger crease the top square along one marked line. Make a small cut through the marked square along the marked line. Insert scissors between the squares and carefully cut along the lines to each corner, making sure you cut through the marked square only. Press the triangles away from the centre square, aligning the points to the marked lines on the wadding. Trim away any fabric 'ears', taking care not to cut the wadding.

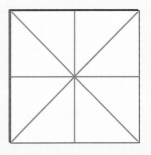

3 **Second Round:** cut each 4¼″ red and green square into four triangles using two diagonal cuts from corner to corner. Place four triangles, two from each colour, right side down on the centre square.

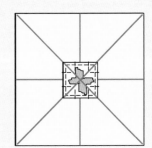
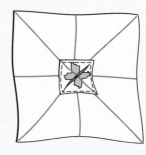
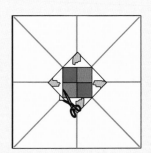
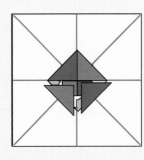
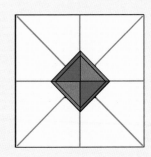

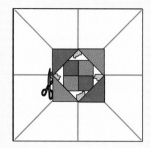

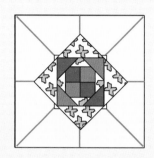

Follow the colour sequence, aligning with the four patch centre.

Triangle points must meet in the centre. Pin well, at right angles to sides of square.

Stitch with a ¼" seam around all four sides. Again, start and finish in the centre of one side.

Press triangles away from centre squares, carefully removing fabric 'ears'.

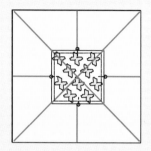

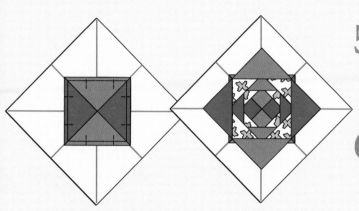

4 **Third Round** is marked and stitched as first round using a 5" square of patterned fabric.

5 **Fourth Round:** repeat step 3 using 6¼" red and green squares cut diagonally into four triangles. Make sure you follow the colour sequence.

6 **Fifth Round:** repeat step 2 using the 8" square of patterned fabric. Sew in place **using a ½" seam.**

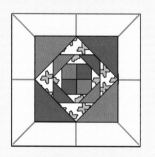

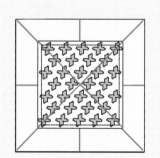

7 **Sixth Round:** repeat step 3 using 9¾" red and green squares cut diagonally into four triangles. Again stitch with a ½" **seam.**

If you are making a multiple block quilt, begin and end the ½" seam with a secure stitch 1½" away from the fabric edges on each side of the square. This unstitched area is necessary to keep the wadding and fabric free when the blocks are joined.

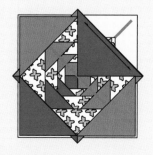

Making Winter Comfort using Quilt as you Go

Fabric required for a 43" × 43" quilt, 10½" finished block size

Neutral/light: 1½ yards

Red and green: ¾ yard each

Backing fabric and cotton wadding: 2½ yards

Cutting the fabrics

Light fabric: 16 × 3½" squares, 16 × 5" squares, 16 × 8" squares.

Red and green fabric: start by cutting the largest squares first. From each fabric cut 32 × 2" squares for four patch.

Cut 4 × 4¼" squares, 4 × 6¼" squares, 4 × 9¾" squares and cut each of these twice to make four triangles from each square.

Backing fabric: cut 16 × 13" squares (you could use two fabrics to give a chequerboard effect quilt back).

Assembling the quilt

Make 16 blocks using the method on pp. 14–15.

Trim the blocks to 12" squares, and trim off a ½" square from each corner.

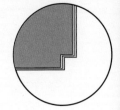

Lay out blocks as in quilt photo below.

Stitch four blocks together in a row using a ½" seam. The seam's raw edges will be on the right side of the quilt. Trim the wadding back to the seam line.

Stitch four rows together, and again trim the wadding back to the seam line, which again will be on the right side of the quilt. ***Do not trim the outside edges of the blocks*** as the wadding needs to go right to the edge, ready for binding.

Bind the quilt.

Snip the raw seams at ½" intervals, then wash and tumble dry the quilt to help create the raggy edge.

Winter Comfort *by Karin Hellaby (43" square, 10½" block). Red, green and cream flannel.*

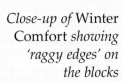

Close-up of Winter Comfort *showing 'raggy edges' on the blocks*

SHELL
UCATION

THE CROSSOVER

Kwame Alexander

Great Works Instructional Guides for Literature

Build students' literacy skills with up-to-date guides for the exploration of rich, complex literature that includes exemplars from the standards, Newbery Medal award-winning titles, classic literature, and popular authors. These guides encourage readers to analyze story elements in multiple ways, boost vocabulary development and writing skills with text-based vocabulary practice and reader-response writing prompts.

Great Works:
Instructional Guides for Literature

8.5" x 11" | 72pp.

Title	ISBN	Item#
Suggested Grade Levels 3–8 Titles		
Because of Winn-Dixie	9781425889555	IFC40218
Charlotte's Web	9781480769953	IFC40219
Freckle Juice	9781480769939	IFC40110
How to Eat Fried Worms	9781480769946	IFC40104
A Wrinkle in Time Newbery	9781425889906	IFC40217
Bridge to Terabithia Newbery	9781425889746	IFC40201
Bud, Not Buddy Newbery	9781425889753	IFC40202
Dragonwings	9781425889777	IFC40204
Esperanza Rising	9781480785120	IFC40224
Flora & Ulysses: The Illuminated Adventures Newbery	9781480782341	IFC40111
Hamilton: An American Musical	9781425816957	IFC51695
Hatchet	9781425889791	IFC40206
Holes Newbery	9781425889807	IFC40207
Island of the Blue Dolphins Newbery	9781425889814	IFC40208
M.C. Higgins, the Great Newbery	9781425889821	IFC40209
Maniac Magee Newbery	9781425889838	IFC40210
My Brother Sam Is Dead	9781425889845	IFC40211
Number the Stars Newbery	9781425889852	IFC40212
Roll of Thunder, Hear My Cry Newbery	9781425889876	IFC40214
The Adventures of Tom Sawyer	9781425889739	IFC40200
The Boy in the Striped Pajamas	9781480785076	IFC40222
The Crossover Newbery	9781425816483	IFC51648
The Dark Is Rising	9781425889760	IFC40203
The Giver Newbery	9781425889784	IFC40205
The Hunger Games	9781480785151	IFC40225
The Lion, the Witch and the Wardrobe	9781480769137	IFC40121
The Watsons Go to Birmingham–1963	9781425889890	IFC40216
Tuck Everlasting	9781425889883	IFC40215
Suggested Grade Levels 9–12 Titles		
Fahrenheit 451	9781425889920	IFC40301
Of Mice and Men	9781480785083	IFC40300
The Great Gatsby	9781425889937	IFC40302
The Odyssey	9781425889944	IFC40303
The Outsiders	9781425889951	IFC40304
Their Eyes Were Watching God	9781425889975	IFC40306
To Kill a Mockingbird	9781425889999	IFC40308

Newbery = Based on Newbery Medal Winner

College & Career Readiness

SHELL EDUCATION

5301 Oceanus Drive • Huntington Beach, CA 92●